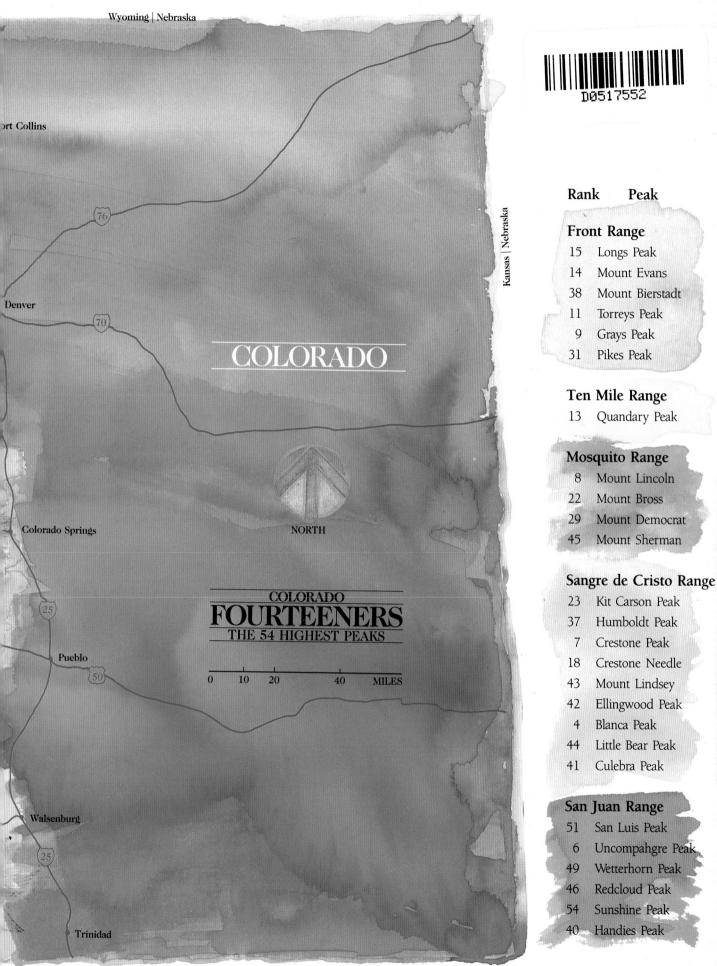

Wyoming | Nebraska

Fort Collins

76

Denver

70

COLORADO

NORTH

Kansas | Nebraska

Colorado Springs

25

Pueblo

50

COLORADO
FOURTEENERS
THE 54 HIGHEST PEAKS

| 0 | 10 | 20 | 40 | MILES |

Walsenburg

25

Trinidad

New Mexico | Oklahoma

Rank	Peak

Front Range
15	Longs Peak
14	Mount Evans
38	Mount Bierstadt
11	Torreys Peak
9	Grays Peak
31	Pikes Peak

Ten Mile Range
| 13 | Quandary Peak |

Mosquito Range
8	Mount Lincoln
22	Mount Bross
29	Mount Democrat
45	Mount Sherman

Sangre de Cristo Range
23	Kit Carson Peak
37	Humboldt Peak
7	Crestone Peak
18	Crestone Needle
43	Mount Lindsey
42	Ellingwood Peak
4	Blanca Peak
44	Little Bear Peak
41	Culebra Peak

San Juan Range
51	San Luis Peak
6	Uncompahgre Peak
49	Wetterhorn Peak
46	Redcloud Peak
54	Sunshine Peak
40	Handies Peak

COLORADO
FOURTEENERS
THE 54 HIGHEST PEAKS

PHOTOGRAPHY AND TEXT BY ROGER EDRINN

WESTCLIFFE PUBLISHERS, INC. ENGLEWOOD, COLORADO

CONTENTS

International Standard Book Number:
ISBN 0-942394-23-2
Library of Congress Catalogue Card Number:
86-050065
Copyright, Photographs and Text: Roger Edrinn,
1986, 1990. All rights reserved.
Book Designer: Gerald Miller Simpson/Denver
Illustrations: Ann Pappageorge
Maps: Ann W. Douden
Typographer: Edward A. Nies
Printed in Korea by Sung In Printing Co., Ltd.,
Seoul
Publisher: Westcliffe Publishers, Inc.
2650 South Zuni Street
Englewood, Colorado 80110

No portion of this book, either photographs or text,
may be reproduced in any form without the written
permission of the publisher.

*First frontispiece: May storm clouds over Mount
Princeton, Sawatch Range.*

*Title page: The characteristic parabolic ridges of the
western Elk Range as seen on the south ridge of
Snowmass Mountain.*

*Right: One of the many falls and cascades along
Kilpacker Creek at the base of El Diente Peak, San
Miguel Range.*

PREFACE

As we begin the last decade of the second millennium, all manner of questions arise as to the future of Spaceship Earth. The recent journeys of Voyager dramatize Earth's uniqueness in our solar system. This book cannot pretend to solve or even raise all the questions so increasingly on our minds. But I believe that the time and exertion necessary to climb one of Colorado's fourteeners does hone an appreciation for the unique treasure we share and must strive to preserve. Living in Colorado and viewing our home from one of its lofty summits makes us keenly aware of the magnificence of our planet.

I completed my first Colorado Grand Slam—climbing all fifty-four of Colorado's fourteeners—in August 1981. By the time I had climbed two or three dozen, I realized I no longer needed a blow-by-blow route description to guide me; a good photograph would have been more than ample. So, in 1981, with no more fourteeners left to challenge me, I began planning a photographic climbing guide with an emphasis on technically superior images.

Since the first printing of this book in 1986, I have reclimbed all fifty-four of the fourteeners and met many interesting people, from first-timers to multiple Grand Slammers. While a few succumb to "peak bagging disease" where the count is more important than the experience, the majority view the climbing of Colorado's highest summits as a healthy exercise for mind and body. I find it particularly enjoyable to see families climbing, sharing the special bonding of playing together. As for me, I almost always climb alone because the staccato nature of my photography does not lend itself to the "got to get to the summit" mind-set that soon develops in even the most selfless companion.

I climb alone, that is, except for my dog, Diente (see page 10), who faithfully follows a hundred yards ahead. Since he is only along for the smells, when or if he gets to the summit is of no great consequence. If my photo stop is short, he simply stands on a high rock or cliff with his ears drooping down and a quizzical look on his face as if to say, "What's holding you up this time?" For longer stops he retraces his steps and lies down nearby with a combined sigh and groan.

Fellow climbers frequently ask me about Diente's climbing ability. The answer is that he knows not that he cannot, therefore he does. No less amazing is that he is alive at all, given his intimate contact with the front bumper of a Vega before his second birthday. This resulted in a compound fracture of the left hip and a permanent metal plate and slightly askew left leg. Diente finished his first Colorado Grand Slam on his eighth birthday, after an effort of a little more than three years. The train ride to Needleton was the significant barrier. In 1989 we reached the Needle Mountains from Purgatory Ski Area, making a forty-mile round-trip hike to avoid the train. To the best of my knowledge, Diente is the only dog to have done a Colorado Grand Slam.

My first Colorado Grand Slam required almost eleven years, the second slightly more than two. The two efforts had many similarities and differences. Most surprising was that I was not in any sense bored the second time around. Whenever possible I chose a different route, a different season, or a different time of day. All of these changes improved the photo opportunities and gave me fresh vistas and a sense of something new.

Reaching the vast majority of summits is no more difficult than finding the trailhead and putting one foot ahead of the other enough times to reach the top. For most summits you can use the one hour per thousand rule: figure on one hour of hiking for each one thousand feet of elevation gain, irrespective of horizontal distance. For very easy roads and trails it is possible to double the gain per hour. If the route is steep and loose, then cut the gain in half.

Because there is some disagreement as to what constitutes a fourteener, a few words are in order. Clearly, if any one point on a mass of rock exceeds 14,000 feet, there is at least one fourteener. The arbitrary rules of man apply if there is a second or third 14,000-foot summit nearby. According to the rule makers—the Colorado Mountain Club and the United States Geological Survey—for the second summit to be counted as an official fourteener it must be one mile from its higher neighbor and have a low point at least five hundred feet below its summit. These rules—evenly applied and barring any historical standing—would net Colorado forty-eight fourteeners. The six peaks that miss one or both criteria are: Ellingwood, Little Bear, North Maroon, Tabeguache, El Diente, and Bross. In spite of the rules, both the CMC and USGS recognize five of the six as official fourteeners, and the CMC additionally accepts Ellingwood.

Crestone Needle from the east summit of Crestone Peak.

Overleaf: Mother Nature at her best on a warm September afternoon at the base of La Plata Peak.

Invariably, the most common question I'm asked by fellow climbers during summit chats is "Which one is the hardest?" The question is simple but the answer is not. There is no definitive answer because of the many variables, such as weather and individual fear factors. All that said, I would be ducking the question not to provide an answer, so here's the final ordering of my yellow stickies:

The Toughest Fourteeners

Summit	Comments
North Maroon	Steep, complicated routes, weak rock
Little Bear	Very steep and wet gully, flying rocks
Capitol	Exposure, generally good rock
Kit Carson	Steep descent from false summit
Crestone Needle	Complicated route, steep problems
Mount Wilson	Steep final pitch, loose large rock
Sunlight	Steep short pitches, solid rock
El Diente	Weak volcanic rock, steep
Pyramid	Steep gullies at treeline
Wetterhorn	Exposed final pitch
Crestone Peak	Easiest via Cottonwood Lake
Wilson Peak	Minor summit ridge exposure
Longs	Long, some exposure, good rock

The easiest fourteener? My vote is Mount Sherman, followed closely by Grays and then Democrat.

While none of the above list are considered technical climbs, especially during summer, rock climbing training is highly recommended. Such training vastly increases confidence and skills for the technical problems sure to be encountered. Confidence is especially important in exposed situations, because knowing you can is 90 percent of doing.

The most unpredictable aspect of Colorado mountaineering is the chance encounter with large wildlife: mule deer, elk, bighorn sheep, mountain goat, and bear. It is the goat, first introduced in Colorado in 1948, that you are most likely to encounter. A number of reasons account for this fortunate circumstance: their white coats, their habitat above treeline, their exposure to lots of people, and their large numbers. If you want to see them up close, from twenty feet or less, sit down. These small creatures—approximately thirty inches at the shoulder—are very curious. If you're patient, they will approach quite near. They are particularly fascinated by small dogs and small children. Your best chances of finding goats are on Bierstadt and Evans, Grays and Torreys, the Sawatch Range from Massive to Shavano, and the Needle Mountains. Bighorn sheep are more numerous and widely distributed than goats, but also shyer and much harder to spot at a distance.

Allow me to impart a little knowledge gleaned from numerous scrapes with Mother Nature. Without a doubt, weather is the greatest barrier to achieving a fourteener summit. Just remember that the summit will be there tomorrow. Will you? On the other hand, if you're always easily turned back by adverse conditions, you may never get on top. Only experience can increase your personal knowledge for making the "right" decision.

After spending a sleepless night under a full moon on the summit of Elbert, I learned that the way to acclimate the body to high-altitude sleeping is by slowly increasing elevation. Unfortunately, this solution doesn't coexist with busy lifestyles. Oh well.

If you're climbing on a cold and windy day and you feel sluggish, consider that you may be borderline hypothermic. To keep from perspiring, you tend to underdress to avoid that wet, chilled feeling when you stop. Instead, wear a light, windproof shell coupled with the clothes necessary to keep warm. If you're breaking a light sweat, you're dressed perfectly.

One experience to avoid is the sensation of electrically induced cobwebs on your face just before the sound of nearby thunder. When you're close enough for every facial hair to stand on end, you're close enough to get hit. If you see the lightning flash--congratulations!!!--you're still alive. If hail is coming down at an inch in ten minutes, it's a probability game. The likelihood of ending up wet, cold, and uncomfortable is very high, but the chance of being struck by lightning is very low. On the other hand, if the odds go against you, the consequences can be severe. You decide.

My equipment to photograph the images in this book were a Pentax 6x7 camera with lenses ranging from 45mm to 300mm, and an assortment of Konica SLR and rangefinder cameras with lenses from 24mm to 400mm. Films used were various Kodak Ektachromes for the 120 format and Kodachrome 25 for the 35mm cameras. Because the quality of light is the single most important element in a successful image, I seldom photograph more than two hours after sunrise or before sunset.

—ROGER EDRINN

The summit of Mount Antero with the photographer on the opposite side of the camera.
(*Roger Riewerts photo*)

FRONT
RANGE

The Front Range is the first set of mountains one sees when approaching Colorado from the east. All six of its fourteeners are less than two hours from Denver and are generally easy climbs; two of them, Evans and Pikes, have automobile roads to their summits.

The most famous peak in this range, and in all of Colorado, is Pikes Peak, named after the early Colorado explorer, Zebulon Pike.

Longs Peak, in Rocky Mountain National Park, is the most dramatic in appearance, and the most difficult to climb. The easiest route involves a five thousand foot elevation gain, some exposed or steep climbing, and a fourteen-mile round trip. The famous vertical east Diamond face offers world-class technical climbs. Longs is the only Colorado fourteener that lies within a national park.

Although Grays and Torreys are probably the easiest to climb, this in no way diminishes their appeal. Look for an old mine at the beginning of the trail, wildflowers along the way, and a 360-degree view from their summits. A goat herd often seen near the summit caps the experience. These are the only fourteeners whose summits straddle the Continental Divide.

Since the Georgetown side of Guanella Pass road is open year-round, Bierstadt offers the possibility of an easy winter climb. The ascent can begin by snowshoeing or skiing over the seemingly impassable willows at the base. These same willows are the primary food source for a large ptarmigan population, so keep your eyes open.

The east side of Mount Evans offers excellent opportunities to view mountain goats along the summit road. They are visible all summer from timberline to near the summit. Leave your vehicle behind to get the closest view; sometimes curiosity will get the better of them, particularly if they spot a child, and the goats will approach people.

MOUNT EVANS (14,264) and MOUNT BIERSTADT (14,060) Evans and Bierstadt as seen from west of Guanella Pass. With its moderate slopes and easy access, Bierstadt is a good winter climb using either snow shoes or skis with climbing skins. The ridge between the two mountains requires technical gear in winter.

LONGS PEAK (14,255) Longs Peaks is the premier peak of the Front Range. Its awesome granite faces, over-hanging rock outcroppings, and distinctive square top make it memorable among Colorado mountains.

Right: PIKES PEAK (14,110) Without a doubt, Pikes Peak is the best known mountain in Colorado. Many visitors assume it is Colorado's highest mountain. The road to the summit, site of the famous Pikes Peak Hill Climb automobile race, and the cog railroad are two distinctive features of Pikes Peak.

Overleaf: GRAYS PEAK (14,270) and TORREYS PEAK (14,267) Grays Peak is a popular first fourteener for many people. It is close to Denver, has a decent road to its base, and has an excellent trail to its summit. One can walk the short ridge to Torreys Peak and have climbed two fourteeners in one day.

TEN MILE
RANGE

Ten Mile Range stretches from Frisco on the north, past Breckenridge on the east, to the Continental Divide between Fremont and Hoosier Passes. It's a short, approximately ten-mile-long range. Many of its summits are numbered instead of named, such as peaks 8, 9, and 10 in Breckenridge Ski Area.

Quandary Peak is the range's only fourteener, although most of the peaks near Quandary are over 13,900 feet and noticeably steeper.

For those who like high ridge hikes, it is possible to get on Ten Mile's ridge just south of Frisco and continue south for over 30 miles, never once dropping below timberline. The traverse will cover the entire Ten Mile Range and most of Mosquito Range, crossing the Continental Divide and both Mosquito and Weston Passes. This adventure, with its occasional thin ridges, is for very strong climbers with some technical skills.

QUANDARY PEAK (14,265)   Quandary offers an excellent winter climb by virtue of its short approach and moderate slopes. It has mining structures on its steep south face which make for interesting exploring for the more ambitious climber. Its summit affords interesting views of South Park and the Blue River Valley.

MOSQUITO
RANGE

The Mosquito Range, with four fourteeners among its many lofty summits, separates the Arkansas River Valley from South Park, extending southward from the Continental Divide to Salida.

The Mosquitoes were home to significant mining activity before the turn of the century. Evidence of placer mining can be seen along the river beds around Fairplay, while many old mines and mills are visible from the climbing routes.

The extensive mineralization has photographic benefits. The rock often has more coloration than the simple grays so common throughout Colorado's ranges. If one can combine these colors with the warmth of the rising or setting sun, spectacular photographs are likely.

Many of the old mine roads are marginally maintained for the numerous visitors to the area. A four-wheel-drive vehicle will ease access to much of this country, but only those on foot can see all that the Mosquitoes have to offer.

All of the range's peaks are easy climbs. Democrat, Lincoln, and Bross are commonly done in one day using the Kite Lake approach. Sherman can be climbed from the Leadville side via a good mine road leading to its base, as well as from the traditional eastern approach.

Yes, the Mosquito Range gets its name for good reason. July is the worst month for mosquitoes . . . it must be the water!

MOUNT SHERMAN (14,036)   Mount Sherman, named after Civil War General William Tecumseh Sherman, is probably the easiest fourteener to climb. Look for evidence of the aerial tram which hauled ore from the 13,000-foot elevation of the nearby Hilltop Mine to below treeline.

Overleaf: MOUNT DEMOCRAT (14,148), MOUNT LINCOLN (14,286) AND MOUNT BROSS (14,172)   These three fourteeners are commonly climbed in one day starting from Kite Lake Campground. From the summit of Democrat one can see the massive Climax Mine, which extracts molybdenum ore from a combination open pit and shaft mine. Mount Cameron, which is higher than either Bross or Democrat, is not considered a separate fourteener, but rather a sub-peak of Lincoln.

SAWATCH
RANGE

The Sawatch (pronounced say-watch) Range is the most central of Colorado's mountain ranges. None of its summits are on the Continental Divide, although they straddle it for over fifty miles. Rising out of the Arkansas River Valley, they are characterized by their broad-shouldered profiles and massive size.

This range has the greatest number of fourteeners, as well as the highest. The three highest peaks in the state, Elbert, Massive, and Harvard, are among the range's fifteen fourteeners.

They are all easy or moderate climbs, with as many routes as the compass has points. The common slopes of fractured granite pack tightly, affording numerous footholds and minimizing the "two steps up, one step down" syndrome common with gravel scree slopes.

One finds numerous places to cross the range in this long, high range straddling the Divide. Sawatch's passes include Hagerman, Independence, Cottonwood, Tincup, Hancock, and Monarch, all over 11,000 feet high. Some are open year-round; others only three months. In addition, there are many lesser passes which can be crossed only on foot. Roads leading to the passes always have views of at least one fourteener.

Secluded wilderness experiences are still possible in the Sawatch, in spite of the relatively easy access its many roads afford. However, heading for one of the range's fourteeners is not, unfortunately, the way to find it.

The Sawatch also contains a subgroup of fourteeners called the "Collegiates": Harvard, Columbia, Yale, and Princeton.

HURON PEAK (14,005) Huron Peak, like many of the peaks of the Sawatch, had a lot of mining activity at its base. The valley to its west is a popular camping spot for four-wheel-drive outings and backpackers. The streams in this area are still good places for gold panners to try their luck.

Overleaf: MISSOURI MOUNTAIN (14,067), MOUNT BELFORD (14,197) and MOUNT OXFORD (14,153) Missouri, Belford and Oxford, along with Huron, are on an east-west spur of the main Sawatch range. This photograph was taken from above 13,000 feet on an unnamed summit jutting northeast from Mount Harvard. The valley between is roadless and offers an excellent backpacking alternative route to reach five fourteeners.

MOUNT SHAVANO (14,229) and MOUNT TABEGUACHE (14,155)   Shavano and Tabeguache offer a good chance of encountering a herd of mountain goats while climbing. It can be a humbling experience to watch them dance through the rocks with the greatest of ease.

Right: MOUNT PRINCETON (14,197)   Mount Princeton dominates the Arkansas valley as no other peak. On the drive west over Trout Creek Pass, its huge hulk commands attention.

LA PLATA PEAK (14,336) Unlike most of the peaks of the Sawatch, La Plata has no roads or mines on or near the mountain. The rock on its summit has decomposed sufficiently to allow for a significant number of flowering plants at the very top. Its only climbing problem is crossing the fast and deep creeks at the base.

Right: MOUNT COLUMBIA (14,073) This photo was taken from across Frenchman Creek and shows the back route used when doing the Harvard-Columbia circle route from Horn Fork Basin. Both peaks are easily climbed from Frenchman Creek.

Overleaf: MOUNT ANTERO (14,269) The Arkansas valley was shrouded in fog the morning this photograph was taken. The challenge is to await the appearance of the summit all the while hoping the lower clouds will remain in sufficient numbers to add interest. The occasional group of golden aspen tips off the time of the year.

MOUNT MASSIVE (14,421) With its multiple summits above 14,000 feet, Mount Massive does not present the classic pyramidal mountain shape. This view from the southwest is not as well-known as the one from Leadville. The west side also offers climbing routes less populated than the Main Range Trail approach.

Right: MOUNT YALE (14,196) Because the Cottonwood Pass road goes south of the summit and there is a lot of semi-open timber, Yale is a good early-season climb. The inexperienced climbers' tendency is to skirt the prominent south false summit to avoid losing some 200 feet. This is a false economy of energy because the steep and loose sides wear down the climber more than regaining the 200 feet.

Overleaf: MOUNT HARVARD (14,420) The northeast side of Harvard showing the summit and most of the ridge to Mt. Columbia. From this vantage point you can see five fourteeners: Columbia, Harvard, Missouri, Belford and Oxford.

MOUNT ELBERT (14,433)   Mount Elbert is Colorado's tallest mountain. It is not a very difficult climb, however, just long. Shortly after World War II a jeep made it to the summit. Today, it is a popular winter trip for strong and experienced cross country skiers.

Right: MOUNT OF THE HOLY CROSS (14,005)   The classic sunrise view is of the cross from Notch Top Mountain. The Forest Service maintains an excellent cabin at the 13,100 foot elevation of Notch Top not far from where this photo was taken. The late 1800 photos of Holy Cross show the right hand arm of the cross to be more complete than today.

ELK RANGE

Running westward from the center of the Sawatch Range is the Elk Range, bisecting the towns of Aspen and Crested Butte. The Elk's six fourteeners are in small clusters, separated by a dozen miles. Its peaks are the classic "rocky mountain high" range, often breathtaking in their grandeur.

Climbing is moderate to difficult on all of the Elk's fourteeners, with route finding on the descent being the principal challenge. For a complex set of reasons, any route looks completely different coming down than going up. Finding a good descent route is especially important during a thunderstorm with the accompanying loss of traction on wet rock and grass. By all means, on the way up one should make mental notes of major changes of direction for one's return.

The biggest problem, however, is that after climbing in the Elks, other ranges will likely seem boring.

The Elk Range offers a great variety of rock from the maroon shales of the Bells and Pyramid to the granite of Capitol and Snowmass. It all requires care and testing, but is not as bad as the rumor mill would have one believe.

PYRAMID PEAK (14,018) Pyramid Peak cannot be seen from Maroon Lake because it is obscured by the false summits north of the peak. This photo was taken approximately 1500 feet above and 1 mile west of the lake. The popular routes go up the steep snow chutes to the north face and then circle around to either the east or west faces.

CAPITOL PEAK (14,130)   The six mile backpack from the end of the road to the base of Capitol has some of the prettiest scenery in Colorado. The mountain is visible almost the entire way and it is impressive. Look forward to one of the most breathtaking climbs and fourteeners in the state.

Right: A view of Capitol with the famous "knife edge" ridge in the foreground. The difficulty of the ridge is highly exaggerated because it has ample hand and foot holds and lack of nearby cliffs to work your psyche. The descent from K2 onto the ridge is far more threatening.

Overleaf: SNOWMASS MOUNTAIN (14,092)   An alternative to the traditional Snowmass Lake and snowfield climb from the east is the view seen here. The approach is through the towns of Marble and Crystal to the Lead King Basin. A backpack to Geneva Lake as a base camp allows for a short hike to Siberia Lake and then a climb up the west ridge to the summit.

MAROON PEAK (14,156) and NORTH MAROON PEAK (14,014)   More popularly known as the Maroon Bells or the Bells, Maroon and North Maroon peak are among the most photographed mountains in Colorado. They are also known as the Deadly Bells to climbers because of the lives they have claimed.

Right: CASTLE PEAK (14,265)   There are more than a half-dozen climbers in the middle part of the photo crossing the snowfields. Their route will take them to the saddle to the right of the summit. An alternative route is to take the rocky ridge to the left of the summit. Just off the photograph on the lower left is the end of the Montezuma Basin four-wheel-drive road which allows easy access to the mountain.

Overleaf: This photograph taken from high on Pyramid Peak shows Snowmass Mountain and Capitol Peak. The trail you see crosses Buckskin Pass to Snowmass Lake on the far side. The photograph demonstrates the variety of rock types present in the Elk Range.

SANGRE DE CRISTO
RANGE

The Sangre de Cristo ("Blood of Christ") Range is long, thin, steep, and high. Running from Salida south to New Mexico, it has nine fourteeners, most of which are visible from the San Luis Valley.

Some of the peaks, such as Humboldt and Culebra, are walk-ups, but others are among Colorado's most challenging. All are made more difficult by the long base approaches. The South Colony Lakes access for the Crestones and the Como Lake access for the Sierra Blanca peaks are two of the roughest four-wheel roads in the state. On a good day, only one in twenty will make it to Como Lake; most jeeps stop two miles earlier where the road turns into a rocky staircase.

Crestone Peak, first climbed by Albert Ellingwood on July 24, 1916, was the last fourteener to be climbed in Colorado. Climber Ellingwood is the same one whose name appears on mountain features throughout the state.

The Crestone group is characterized by conglomerate rock. Its rounded river boulders have been bound together under intense heat and pressure, upthrust, and re-eroded, graphically displaying the multiple building phases of the eons.

The dominant southwest winds and the location of three low passes between the Crestones and the Sierra Blanca peaks have combined to create the highest sand dunes in North America. The towering Crestones make for an interesting contrast with the soft, rounded dunes at the entrance to Sand Dunes National Monument.

Throughout the range are many displays of the state flower, the columbine. It grows profusely here in late July, near timberline.

BLANCA PEAK (14,345) Blanca Peak is a very difficult climb from the Huerfano River Basin shown in this photograph. The popular route today is from the Como Lake Basin west of the summit.

KIT CARSON PEAK (14,165)   This view of Kit Carson is from the summit of Crestone Peak. Kit Carson is most commonly climbed from the South Colony Lakes by going over the 13,800 false summit. Another less popular route is the Spanish Creek access from the town of Crestone on the west. This is an easier route for Kit Carson because it avoids the false summit.

Right: HUMBOLDT PEAK (14,064)   This view of Humboldt is from the north side of Crestone Needle looking east over Upper South Colony Lake. Humboldt is a steep walk up a grassy slope. The views from Humboldt of the Crestones are spectacular.

CRESTONE NEEDLE (14,197)   An example of the beautiful columbine that flourish at the base of the Crestones. The ridge coming straight at the camera is the Ellingwood Arete, named after Albert Ellingwood, pioneer climber of the Crestones. The "pedestrian" route makes use of the ridge on the left skyline.

Right: CRESTONE PEAK (14,294)   When it comes to naming the toughest fourteener in Colorado, Crestone Peak is invariably at or near the top of everyone's list. It is both technically and physically demanding. Those demands reward one with a tremendous feeling of satisfaction upon successfully completing the climb.

Overleaf: The view of Crestone Needle and the ridge leading to Crestone Peak from the southwest side of Humboldt. The photograph was taken on a cold, clear morning in late October. From this point it is a short hike to the Bears Playground, the flat triple junction of Humboldt, Crestone Peak, and Kit Carson.

MOUNT LINDSEY (14,042)   Mount Lindsey as seen from the summit of Blanca, with morning storm clouds building. Because of the closed private land to the south, Lindsey is almost always climbed from the Huerfano River drainage. The summit route takes one across the left skyline ridge.

Right: ELLINGWOOD PEAK (14,042)   Briefly mentioned in the preface as the controversial fourteener, it is another Colorado mountain feature named after Albert Ellingwood. Ellingwood is commonly climbed with Blanca from the Como Lake Basin. It is less than an hour from the summit of Blanca to Ellingwood's summit.

CULEBRA PEAK (14,047) Culebra is the only Colorado fourteener on private land. Along with much of the land in this part of the state, Culebra was part of old land grants totaling millions of acres. This view of the summit is from the west false summit looking east. The whole mountain can be readily seen from the road between Fort Garland and San Luis.

Right: LITTLE BEAR PEAK (14,037) This view of Little Bear from the summit of Ellingwood shows a mountain lake slowly shedding its winter coat of snow in early July. The flat area behind the peak is the San Luis Valley near Alamosa.

SAN JUAN
RANGE

The San Juan Range, the most massive range in both land area and average height, dominates the southwest corner of Colorado. So great is its size that on a clear day from the high point on 14,309-foot Uncompahgre Peak, its furthest mountains look like bluish ant hills. The range marks the most westerly advance of the Continental Divide.

The area's four-wheel-drive road system allows relatively easy access to mountain bases. These roads exist because of the intense mining activity from the 1880s on. Although many are maintained by county crews, many others are in various stages of decay.

The fourteeners centered around Lake City are generally easy to moderate, and the vistas from their summits are truly awe-inspiring toward the south-west. The last thousand feet of the Wetterhorn offers the only exposed climbing.

The other ranges of the San Juans that contain fourteeners are the Needles, Sneffels, and San Miguels.

The northeastern portion is the driest area of the San Juans, and shows much past volcanic activity. Of further geologic interest is Slumgullion Slide, southeast of Lake City. The slide resulted from an entire mountain side breaking away and slipping thousands of feet into the valley below, where it dammed a river to form Lake San Crisobal, Colorado's largest natural lake.

The slide began over a thousand years ago and continues to this day. Its constant motion is apparent where the highway crosses the slide area.

The summit of Uncompahgre showing the sheer northeast face. This face is seldom seen from below unless one backpacks in from the north. As the highest peak in the San Juans, the view from its summit is almost like a view from an airplane.

Overleaf: WETTERHORN PEAK (14,015) and UNCOMPAHGRE PEAK (14,309) Just 300 feet lower than Uncompahgre, Wetterhorn looks dramatically smaller than its neighbor. The two points in between are Matterhorn Peak and an unnamed sub-peak of Uncompahgre.

This view from the summit of Handies looks southwest to the Grenadiers and Needles, the most rugged part of the San Juans. The foreground foliage shows the diversity of flowers common to the San Juans.

Right: HANDIES PEAK (14,048)   This is Handies as seen from deep in American Basin to the west of the summit. It is one of two popular climbing routes to the summit. The other route is from the north, just across the road from the trailhead up Redcloud and Sunshine.

REDCLOUD PEAK (14,034) and SUNSHINE PEAK (14,001)   Because the climbing of these two peaks is largely unexciting, plan to view the variety and abundance of flowers which are characteristic of the San Juans. The surfaces of both peaks are covered with loose scree which is great for going down, less so for going up.

Right: SAN LUIS PEAK (14, 014)   If one can figure out which of the many soft summits is San Luis, then the climb is trivial. Nearby Stewart peak is only some 30 feet lower and is often mistaken for San Luis. This photograph, taken high above and north of Stewart Creek, should help minimize the confusion.

NEEDLE
MOUNTAINS

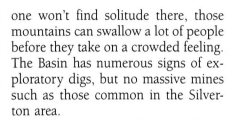

The Needles are among the most remote mountains in Colorado, and are certainly the most remote fourteeners. The area is green and gorgeous, since it receives an extraordinary amount of moisture.

Fortunately for the climber, the three Needle fourteeners are among the easiest of their members. Even so, they have a difficult rating, particularly during southwestern Colorado's "monsoon" season.

A unique aspect of the Needles is their access via a ride on the narrow gauge train from Silverton or Durango. The ride is a long morning from Durango or a short afternoon from Silverton to the "depot" at Needleton. From there it's a six-mile backpack to the base of the peaks in Chicago Basin. Another access is a long backpack from the Vallecito Creek drainage over Columbine Pass, southeast of the Needles.

Chicago Basin is a very popular backpack destination. In fact, talking to the train's conductor one would expect it to be Grand Central Station. While one won't find solitude there, those mountains can swallow a lot of people before they take on a crowded feeling. The Basin has numerous signs of exploratory digs, but no massive mines such as those common in the Silverton area.

The backpack to the lower part of Chicago Basin is a fairly easy hike on an old wagon road which has long since become a wide foot trail. The elevation gain is about two thousand feet in six miles.

From the Basin, a very steep path leads to the twin lakes and cabin in between the three summits. At an elevation of 12,500 feet, the lakes with their flower-covered grassy slopes invite visitors to park their bottom and enjoy the 360-degree panorama of high mountains. But goal-oriented climbers push eastward for the summits of Sunlight, Windom, or westward to Eolus. Eolus is sometimes spelled Aeolus and, in fact, the brass USGS summit marker uses that spelling.

WINDOM PEAK (14,082)   It's difficult to find any distinction among the fourteeners of the Needle Mountains. They are all difficult climbs, have similar rock, and are accessed from the Chicago Basin. The rock offers many hand and foot holds, but it is not particularly stable.

SUNLIGHT PEAK (14,059)   The photographer is ascending the final rock knob of Sunlight.
Climbing legend has it that some brave soul did a hand stand on this knob in spite of the
thousand foot drop off to the left. The large rounded blocks of granite seen here are unique
to Sunlight and only found on its summit. *(Paul Beiser photo)*

Right: MOUNT EOLUS (14,083)   This foggy view of Eolus shows the summit ridge from the
saddle between Eolus' two summits. The left or east side is the easiest route to the summit.
The long, thin summit is approximately 100 by 10 feet with many steep ravines descending
to the valley below.

SNEFFELS
RANGE

Stretching some twenty miles from Ouray on the east to Placerville on the west is the Sneffels Range. Its one fourteener, Mount Sneffels, ranks with Maroon Bells as the two Colorado fourteener groups most likely to appear on a calendar or placemat.

Having but one fourteener in no way diminishes the range's appeal. Its north slope is characterized by precipitous mountains rapidly changing to gently sloped mesas of spruce, aspen, and scrub oak. In the fall, this is one place that combines golden aspen, red scrub oak, and snow-capped peaks during the late September change of seasons, making it a photographer's dream.

The northern side also offers winter enjoyment because of the all-weather highway running east to west over Dallas Divide. The gentle slopes and grand scenery are a magnet for both cross-country skiers and snowmobilers. Just east of Dallas Divide is an especially scenic spot where a zig-zag fence provides a foreground for Mount Sneffels.

The range's southern side is equally accessible from Placerville to Telluride, but only one road runs from Ouray to Telluride, and it is often closed by snowfall accumulations until August. This road is four-wheel-drive only, and crosses 13,100-foot Imogene Pass.

Yankee Boy and Governor Basins, southeast of Mount Sneffels, put on incredibly beautiful flower displays in July and August. Expect to see acres of two-foot high columbine, intermixed with red, yellow, and fuchsia Indian paintbrush, as well as scores of other varieties.

East of Mount Sneffels and north of Yankee Boy Basin is the unusual Teakettle Mountain, which looks just like it should, complete with a natural stone arch for a handle. The teakettle silhouette can be seen only from the south.

MOUNT SNEFFELS (14,150) Sneffels is commonly climbed from either the south, using Blue Lakes as a starting point, or from Yankee Boy Basin. Both routes use the same final approach just east of Blue Lakes Pass.

SAN MIGUEL
RANGE

The San Miguels stretch from Lizard Head on the east to an indeterminant ending in the high mesa country east of the Utah border. The lone volcano cones develop an interesting pattern as they drift off to the west. From the summits of the fourteeners, one sees the La Sal mountains of southeastern Utah on the western horizon.

The poetic sound of the name envelopes one in a sense of beauty and tranquility. High above Wilson Mesa at the base of Silver Pick Basin is perhaps the most beautiful spot in Colorado. It's surrounded by the snow-clad mountains of the Sneffels, San Juan, and San Miguel ranges. In early June, deer graze off tender aspen shoots, and the setting sun turns it a crimson red.

The San Miguels offer two of Colorado's most difficult peaks: El Diente and Mount Wilson. Adjacent Wilson Peak, while not as difficult, can also be a challenge, especially if one encounters ice on the ridge coulee.

In spite of their difficulty, a very strong party can do all three summits in one day. But for those who choose to hold down the summit with their bottom side for at least an hour, no day is long enough.

The west ridge of El Diente, which looks so inviting on the topographic maps, offers a knife edge that would put Capitol's to shame. Mount Wilson and El Diente are both best climbed via the ridge between the two summits. This ridge has the reputation of one of the hardest fourteener ridges in Colorado, so calling it the "best" route makes sense only in relation to the other choices. The ridge is a feast of colors, with yellow-green lichen contrasting with the reddish-brown volcanic rock.

A rewarding route for both El Diente and Mount Wilson is from Kilpacker Falls until early summer; when the snow finally recedes, the base is a prime viewing spot for columbine wildflowers.

EL DIENTE PEAK (14,159) Columbine, Colorado's state flower, flowers at the base of El Diente in early September. The west ridge (on the skyline to the left of the summit) of El Diente, which looks so inviting on a USGS quad map, offers a true knife-edge to add spice to an otherwise difficult route.

WILSON PEAK (14,017)   Wilson Peak is the most photographed of the two Wilsons, because it has so many attractive faces. Its climbing routes use Navajo Basin or go past the many mine structures of the Silver Pick Basin just beyond the right ridge.

Right: MOUNT WILSON (14,246)   This view of Mount Wilson from the north side of the summit of El Diente gives some idea of the difficulty of the ridge between the two summits. The most common approach is from Navajo Basin, combining the climb of Mount Wilson with Wilson Peak and El Diente. Another route for Mount Wilson and El Diente is from the south using the Kilpacker Creek approach.

COLORADO'S FOURTEENERS BY RANGE

Rank	Range, Peak, Height (ft.)		Photo Page	Date	Log Notes
	Front Range				
15	Longs Peak	14,255	14	_____	_____
14	Mount Evans	14,264	12	_____	_____
38	Mount Bierstadt	14,060	12	_____	_____
11	Torreys Peak	14,267	16,17	_____	_____
9	Grays Peak	14,270	16,17	_____	_____
31	Pikes Peak	14,110	15	_____	_____
	Ten Mile Range				
13	Quandary Peak	14,265	18	_____	_____
	Mosquito Range				
8	Mount Lincoln	14,286	22,23	_____	_____
22	Mount Bross	14,172	22,23	_____	_____
29	Mount Democrat	14,148	22,23	_____	_____
45	Mount Sherman	14,036	20	_____	_____
	Sawatch Range				
53	Mount of the Holy Cross	14,005	39	_____	_____
2	Mount Massive	14,421	34	_____	_____
1	Mount Elbert	14,433	38	_____	_____
5	La Plata Peak	14,336	8,9,30	_____	_____
27	Mount Oxford	14,153	26,27	_____	_____
19	Mount Belford	14,197	26,27	_____	_____
36	Missouri Mountain	14,067	26,27	_____	_____
52	Huron Peak	14,005	24	_____	_____
3	Mount Harvard	14,420	36,37	_____	_____
35	Mount Columbia	14,073	31	_____	_____
21	Mount Yale	14,196	35	_____	_____
20	Mount Princeton	14,197	2,29	_____	_____
10	Mount Antero	14,269	10,32,33	_____	_____
26	Mount Tabeguache	14,155	28	_____	_____
17	Mount Shavano	14,229	28	_____	_____
	Elk Range				
12	Castle Peak	14,265	47	_____	_____
47	Pyramid Peak	14,018	40	_____	_____
50	North Maroon Peak	14,014	46	_____	_____
25	Maroon Peak	14,156	46	_____	_____
30	Capitol Peak	14,130	42,43,48,49	_____	_____
32	Snowmass Mountain	14,092	3,44,45,48,49	_____	_____